Gut the Ghost

Catherine Merritt

ISBN: 979-8-218-59450-3

Printed in the United States of America

Author photo by Becky Duffyhill Photography

For everyone who has ever been told their softness was weakness.

"Without tenderness, we are in hell."
-Adrienne Rich

CONTENTS

III: THE AFTERLIFE

I:

THE HAUNTING

INK STAIN

I might be the villain in your story,
and you are the monster in mine.

Yet only one of us is brave enough
to pick up a pen
and write the truth.

LOVE-STARVED

They're giving out medals for self-restraint
but I want to win a prize for wanting.
A first place blue ribbon grand prize
for loving until my teeth ache.

I want so desperately to be wanted.
We aren't supposed to say that part out loud,
yet lately I've been fighting the urge
to scream it from every rooftop I see.

Rebecca says adoration is love without expectation,
so how is it I have built cathedrals
out of expectations so high they reach the sun?
Maybe this has always been my undoing
but I will keep on doing it
because my heart does not know
any other way of existing.

Love is an offering designed for consumption,
like a wine-soaked sacrament placed
on your tongue at the altar of affection.
It's an orange in July,
split and shared with all the white bits peeled off.

Love is meant to be consumed, and I am starving.

HEADRUSH

I thought love was mending the broken pieces
no matter how many times they shattered.

I lost so much blood trying to fix
what wasn't mine to mend.

I HATE YOU FOR MAKING ME ROMANTICIZE NEW JERSEY

For the first time I smoked a cigarette
trying to impress you.

For driving up and down the turnpike
and back again.

For boardwalk sunburns on beaches
you pay to walk on.

Always on your terms, never on mine.

For convincing me that mercy filled the space
between my body and your closed fist,
and love could grow there.

MUTUAL DESTRUCTION

If only you knew how many times
I tried to claw my insides out,
hoping the sting of blood
would dull the ache in my bones.

When I shattered and you stepped
on my broken pieces,
ground me into dust,
extinguished me like an old cigarette,
I hoped you would burn yourself on my ashes,
cut yourself on my jagged edges.

Impenetrable skin, impenetrable heart.
Armor on the outside and within.
If only I had been so well protected.

THE PROPHECY

Your mother said one day
I would get sick of you,
so I did not pretend to be surprised
when you put poison in my drink,
held my chin while I swallowed,
and blame me as I lay dying.

HEAD VS. HEART

You would tell anyone else to leave,
yet you are the continuous exception
to your own rules. Always understanding,
always armed with the benefit of the doubt
by the handful, overflowing from pockets
ready to give out whenever she needs them.

She is always sorry.
She always loves you.
        (At least those are her words)

Her actions are this:
        doors slammed, books thrown,
        fist raised to the sky like a comet.

In every photo you wear a smile like a lie.

You feel your bones crush under the weight
of each day you continue to stay.

LAST TRAIN FROM NEW YORK

The first time I said "I love you"
and meant it how you wanted,
in front of rows of strangers
heading home to parents,
to lovers,
and next to me:
                    you.

Tears rolling down my cheeks
like lighter fluid,
and in your hand:
                    a match.

CRUELTY WAS ALWAYS YOUR THING, BUT I'LL TAKE IT FROM HERE

Let me try to be mean about it,
just this once. Let me say
that I hope you're still
living at home with your parents
and working that miserable job
with the creepy old boss
and drinking yourself to sleep.

Let me say for certain
that if I ever saw you again
I wouldn't hesitate
to walk right up to you
and name what you did.
To tell you to go fuck yourself.
But one time, before I moved away,
I thought I saw your car on the highway
and my chest got so tight
I had to pull over.

I guess the most I can do
is write this poem.
I guess the worst I can say
is I wish I never met you.

That I wish I could scrub you clean
from my memory like kitchen tile.
But it's like when they tell you not
to use bleach on black mold because it
only removes the surface stains while the toxins
continue to grow underneath.

It's like no matter how hard I scrub,
no matter how long I spend on bruised knees,
I'm still breathing you in.

I wish I could burn it all down and start over,
but I cannot get rid of my body
and I am done destroying myself for you.

Catherine Merritt

MERLOT

My closet is full of shirts
with sleeves stained red,
remnants of a thing I tried
so hard to give
but no one wanted.
Wine stain blooms mark
the unerasable memory
of old wounds.

The inventor of that phrase
forgot to mention how tender,
how gruesome it is
to rip your own heart from your chest.
To put it on display.
They offered no instructions
on how to sew yourself back up.

I don't remember who taught me
that pain at my own expense
was worth someone else's pleasure,
yet it is ingrained in my brain
with a permanence I cannot rewire.

If I gave enough,
I would be worthy,
I would be good.
I am so tired of being good.

All goodness ever got me was
blood-soaked sleeves
and a closet full of clothes
I can't wear anymore.

GUT THE GHOST

I finally threw away the t-shirt I was wearing when it happened. The soft purple cotton sat in the donation pile in the trunk of my car for months, following me around like a ghost until I decided that it would be bad karma to pass it along to anyone else. I felt guilty throwing it away – wasteful. I think Mother Earth will forgive me this time. I still need to work on forgiving myself.

I kept the sweatshirt you hated out of spite. The one I bought on my birthday when you sat impatiently on the changing room bench. The one I loved, and you hated simply because I loved it. I can't wear it anymore. Too many unpleasant memories woven into the fabric. It still hangs in the back of my closet like a small symbol of resistance. It feels brave to defy you, even in your absence.

I deleted every picture of us. Opened up frames and ripped each photo into tiny shreds over the trashcan. Watched them fall like confetti. Last week my mom asked if I could send her that picture you took of me at the lake, said she loves my smile and the way the light brings out the green in my eyes. I told her I would try to find it, knowing it was already long gone. She couldn't remember your name when she asked about it, just "that girl you used to be friends with." *Friends.* I'm jealous she can't remember your name because even though it's been two years, I still tense up when I hear it. A few months ago I opened a new book only to find that one of the characters shared your name. I snapped it shut like Pandora's box, hoping I could keep the memories from slithering out if I just held the pages tight enough.

I moved out of the apartment where the police came the night you got me so drunk I couldn't stand. You scolded me for the tiniest drop of whiskey left unfinished, and oh how I hate to let anyone down. I tossed it back and paid for it in bruised knees on cold linoleum. The landlord said they were renovating before renting to someone new. Do they know it's haunted there? Know the walls hold echoes of screaming matches? Know the carpet is stained with tears, with blood? Maybe when they gut the kitchen they'll gut the ghost of you, too.

I sold the couch where we spent every weekend drinking too much cheap wine and watching bad movies. It wouldn't fit through the door of my new apartment. The universe's way of reminding me you're not allowed in this new home I've built. It was the biggest physical memory of you that followed me across state lines. Do you know there's a piece of you in Colorado now? Some couple from the internet paid me four hundred dollars for it, reparations they didn't even know they were making on your behalf. When they loaded it into their truck there was laughter instead of yelling. Love feels so much lighter in mile high air.

My first therapist – the one you didn't want me to see – had to be the one to tell me it was abuse. I thought about the night you raised your hand to me in the parking lot. Hot shame at the pleading thought that flickered through my mind. *Please hit me. Maybe then someone will believe me.* My second therapist helped me name what you did out loud. The first time she told me she believed me I cried so hard I couldn't breathe.

I have new friends now. They don't make fun of the way my voice pitches up when I'm anxious. They tell me they love me without expecting anything in return. I have a cat you would hate because you'd accuse me of loving him more than you, and you would be right. I don't think he would like you, either. I have tattoos you'll never see – scars left by choice. "To be soft is to be powerful" etched into my ribcage. A permanent reminder that sensitivity is a virtue, not a weakness.

I've gone on other dates since that Valentine's Day where I cried in the bathroom of the fancy restaurant. I've kissed other girls who have handled me with such tenderness it hurt, but it did not hurt, and that is the point. Love is not supposed to be violent and possessive and vengeful. I know that now.

I read somewhere once that our bodies completely regenerate themselves every seven years. Every cell from our eyelashes to our esophagus becomes new. If it's true, then I only have five more years until I become someone you never knew, never touched.

I'm still counting down the days.

II:

THE EXORCISM

HOW TO PERFORM AN EXORCISM

i. Accept that the body is cold. You cannot bring it back. Accept that you spent months trying to revive a bloodless heart. In the end, you lost the body but saved yourself.

ii. Throw the t-shirt in the dumpster and move 1,714 miles west. Drive through lightning storms and into clean air. Breathe.

iii. Sell the couch and lose 300 pounds of regret in an instant. The body is gone and now so is its ghost.

iv. Say the words out loud. When you can't say it out loud, write it down. Cry until you can't breathe. Let your tears become holy water.

v. Oil the hinges of your heart and pry it open. Let her in. Feel the sun warm you in places you never thought would see light again.

vi. Remember: there is nothing holier or more sacred than love.

(NOT) THE END (YET)

In the beginning my first aid skills were muscle memory.
I picked your teeth out one by one from my skin
and severed the cord that tethered me
to the city with gray skies and gray people.
I discovered that even though my legs were bruised
they still worked enough to carry me
from skyscrapers to mountain views.
The distance between me and that girl
is two therapists, two years, a thousand miles.
I try to trace the line back to her so I can tell her.

Tell her she's going to kiss other girls,
make other friends.
Tell her she'll move to another state,
go hours without checking her phone
if she doesn't want to.
She won't come back to missed calls
or angry texts because she doesn't
belong to anyone but herself.

In the end she goes on good dates
and bad dates and she ghosts dates.
She watches the movie and listens to the song
and hears the name and breathes.
Just breathes.

In the end her first aid skills are rusty,
and she is glad to have forgotten
how to mend her own wounds.

TO BE TENDER

The one time I dare grow thorns
for my own protection
I bore the blame for your blood lost,
so I clipped the thorns one by one
and watched carnations bloom in their wake.

Which is to say:
> you tried to harden me
> but I only grew softer.

I know now that to be tender is not to be weak.
A permanent reminder etched into my ribs,
tucked close to my heart for safe keeping
in a place where you can't touch me anymore.

Soft like sugar-spun confections
and hand-me-down sweaters.
Gentle like her hands when she holds
my face and calls me pretty.

I am soft enough to know that your armor
was a papier mache attempt to soothe your own pain,
but smart enough to know that doesn't excuse
violence inflicted on love's behalf.

My softness saved me
when you tried to break me
because soft things can't shatter.

Tenderness has saved me
time and time again.

EMERGENCY UMBRELLA

I want to be the moon
bathed in an iridescent glow.
Adored each night simply for existing
in all my forms.

I long to be the sun
edged in flecks of gold,
nourishing tulip fields
with my warmth.

Most days I feel like a rainstorm.
Nice to watch when you're dry
and safe inside, but no one wants
to risk getting wet.

ROSEWATER

Cut me open and I bleed love like rosewater.
I'm sorry that it spilled on your shoes
and stained the cracks in the kitchen tiles
but I hope your morning coffee comes out perfect
and you hit all the green lights on the way to work.
I can't stop picking at the hole in my shirt sleeve
because nobody ever taught me how to leave
well enough alone. I revisit old lovers like gravestones
and their ghosts haunt me home.
It's like loving is muscle memory
and I can't stop moving so I walk circles
around my feelings until I've got blisters on my heels.
You're not home yet so I bandage up my own wounds
and scrub the kitchen floor until it sparkles.

BITE

I try not to be angry
when my cat crawls onto my chest,
snuggles in close to my face,
and bites my nose.

I am no stranger to the desire for
affection at any cost.

I too have bared my teeth for love.

HANDLE ME

I envy surgeons' hands:
steady, stable, lifesaving.
The reiki healer who transmits
energy through their fingertips
without ever even touching skin.

My own hands are never still,
turning over stone after stone
until the polish is chipped.
Picking until I see blood.

I have never known when enough is enough
and I pay the price every single time.
My hands have never been steady or quick,
and they are gentle to everyone but me.

ROT

I feel like a ghost of myself
on the days when I let flowers
bought in the name of self care
rot away on the coffee table,
their stems disintegrating in the vase.
My cat meows at the corners of my room,
begging me to get out of bed.
I'm sorry. Existing is too much today.
Maybe tomorrow I'll get up,
refresh the flowers, scoop the litter box.
For now I'll pull the covers up, close my eyes,
and wait to feel human again.

BOTANIST

I have to believe something good
will come of this ache.

Perhaps the tears that stain my sheets
will one day water wildflowers.

May I grow a whole garden
from this pain.

I HEARD YOU FOUND JESUS IN A NEW JERSEY SWIMMING POOL

I am up late again looking in places I shouldn't. I am quick to blame myself since you are not here to do it for me. The water can't be more than three feet deep. A shallow, chlorinated pool of false redemption. Did you hold your nose as they tipped you back? Did you emerge feeling clean? Forgiven? For your sake I hope there is a god and she is as unrelenting as you were. I hope you spent the last four years on knees more bruised than my own, begging for mercy. I hope when you get to her gate she tells you that you got the password wrong and turns you back. Maybe you can try again in another life where we are finally strangers.

ANALOG

I don't want to post this poem online but I don't know how else to reach you. If I send a letter will you read it? Unstick my thoughts and fold open my words. Lay them out across the kitchen table with the coffee stains and trace your finger across each carefully crafted shape. Read between the lines (and the margins, too). Please don't toss me out with the junk mail.

Every scribbled word is a tiny piece of my soul and I can't bear to send such sacredness out into the ether only to get swallowed by an algorithm that cares more about likes than living.

I want to cup my friends' faces in my hands and drink directly from the stream and scream into the sky until my throat is red and raw. I want to go days without looking at my own reflection. Let me stand close enough to see every line and pore on your face without a filter. Show me yours and I'll show you mine. Sit with me and watch the sunset. Leave your phone at home. It still happens even if you don't post it. I am so bored of perfectly curated feeds and photos meticulously arranged and retaken in a feigned attempt at authenticity because being authentic is "in" now.

I want the real thing. The off-screen thing. The chipped-tooth smiles and the conversations that keep me up all night and I want to never answer another email again. I am trying to reach for your hand but this screen keeps getting in my way.

Can you come closer, please?

DEADLY FLIRTATION

I let myself flirt with death
but everyone knows I'm just a tease.
I only want a little taste.
To swallow just enough
to trick myself into being satisfied
before I spit her back out.
Sometimes I have to force her from my mouth,
pry her from my throat with messy fingers
when I get ahead of myself.
I try not to let death into my bed,
but some days she is just so persuasive,
and I am just so tired.

I MADE IT TO 9:15AM WITHOUT CRYING TODAY (AND THAT'S A NEW RECORD)

I worry I am only a good poet
when I am sad
or heartbroken
or in love.

Right now I am all three
at the same time,
so perhaps I am the best poet
I have ever been.

III:

THE AFTERLIFE

Catherine Merritt

IT'S JUNE & I'M LETTING THE LIGHT IN

Watching it scatter into rainbow fractals
through the window pane. Letting it dance
across my kneecaps in the morning breeze.
Kaleidoscope shards that bathe me in color.
Ultraviolet. I don't remember the first time
I heard the word "lesbian" but I remember
the hot blush that bloomed crimson on my cheeks
the first time I saw Willow and Tara kissing on tv.
The recognition that stirred in me. *Oh, yes.*
That is me. Labels aren't for everyone
but this one feels like it was born in me.
A flag in shades of pink, orange, violet.
Summer sunsets you can wrap yourself up in.
It's June and I'm letting the light in.
It is beautiful here.

HOMEGROWN

I am running full speed toward the things that I love and leaving trails of lavender in my wake. The summer air is wet tonight and I am drinking it all in. Open mic night in the living room and queer movies in the backyard. Let me tell you who I am and for once I won't qualify it, won't make myself small. I will tell you about my stories and for the first time I won't feel like I'm faking it. I am finally here. In the thick of it, this life. This soft, precious thing I have created with my own two hands. It's vanilla bean and cherry sweet and I am eating it straight from the vine. Happiness tastes best homegrown. My heart is a tender little thing but I am learning to be brave and let other people hold it. I am learning how good it feels to be held. Learning I don't have to hold it all myself. My hands are empty and my palms are itching with possibility. What else can I grab now? What else can I hold? Give me big messy fistfuls of it and watch me shape it into something magnificent. There is dirt under my nails from forging my own path but I'll paint them with glitter and watch them sparkle in the sun.

BE GENTLE WITH DELICATE THINGS

The seasons are changing and so am I.
I'm shedding conventions like maple leaves
and crunching them under my feet.
I need a haircut and a new tattoo
and somewhere to put my tender heart.

The morning air is getting cold but her hands are warm
and something about September feels like home.
I'll hang the summer flowers up to dry
in the windowsill and watch them bathe
in the golden afternoon light.

The husk of August is hollow now.
Autumn reminds me to be gentle
with delicate things, with myself.

SATIATE

I want to be brave enough to love
and let others love me back.
To let that love crack me wide open.
To bare everything for love.
There is always an end, that is certain,
but perhaps let that certainty be a comfort,
not a fear. Let it propel me forward,
holding white-knuckled to
the very best bits of it all.

I want to be brave enough to live
the messiest life possible, full of love
and heartbreak and tears and joys so big
and soft I can wrap myself up in them like a blanket,
jump from the rooftop because I know
I have a soft place to land.

I have spent so many years biting my nails
over the worst case scenario,
imagining the ways in which
I would disappoint people,
becoming more comfortable disappointing myself.

I have grown so tired of making myself small,
of folding myself into the tiniest squares
to fit neatly into the jeans pocket of someone
who will only forget I'm there
and throw me into the wash like an afterthought.

At the end of the day, it's my life.
It's my heart and my joy and my tears.
It's mine – all mine.

I will let myself be greedy
and eat up every last crumb.

CARTOGRAPHER

The days are getting shorter so I'm lighting
the good candles and taking up cartography.
Which is to say I'm drawing the map
back to myself by hand, this time in pencil.

I decide where the trails bend,
where to pivot and go back.
I can take the long way, the scenic route,
and still get there in the end.

I decide where the end is.
 Maybe I'll decide there is no end.

After all,
          I am nothing if not unfinished

BON APPÉTIT

Dinner at her house is warm and candle-lit / We smoke a
joint on the porch and she sets out the fancy cheese and
crackers even though we're both wearing sweats / No one
talks about calories / She kisses me while we wait for the
water to boil / We get distracted making love on the kitchen
counter / Eat cross-legged on the living room floor until my
foot falls asleep / I've never felt so at ease / So held by the
mere presence of someone / No rush to clean up the plates /
Let the cat lick them clean, she says / I follow her upstairs for
dessert

I AM SO HAPPY I LEFT MY HEART OPEN SO YOU COULD FIND YOUR WAY IN

I have never known a love
I didn't have to ask for,
didn't have to beg
on bruised knees for,
contort myself
into impossible shapes for.
I have never known a love
without conditions until her.

What does it say about me,
having excused unimaginable cruelty
for the chance to feel wanted?
I don't know what love looks like
without claw marks, without
white knuckles and chipped teeth.

But her love, *oh.*
Her love is as soft and tender
as my own heart.
I am still getting used to it,
this love without strings.
I am learning I don't need to hold it so tightly,
learning how to unclench my fists, to breathe.

I don't remember the last time my heart
felt this light, this helium-high and floating
like an afternoon sunbeam.
Like that warm spot where the January sun
hits the hardwood and the cat curls up,
content for an afternoon nap.
Yes, to love her is to finally rest.

AMONGST THE WILDFLOWERS
For Dylah

How lucky am I to be loved by the sun.
To kiss the freckles on your eyelids
as we fall asleep, to feel your fingers
laced in mine like a promise.
Whenever I see wild geese
I will always think of Mary Oliver and you.
Of stretches of side roads, your daughter
asleep in the backseat.
It is the easiest thing I have ever done,
loving you. Like muscle memory, like relief.
I hope I am lucky enough to love you
in every lifetime. Amongst every sprig
of lavender, amongst every wildflower.

CENTER OF THE UNIVERSE
For our daughter

She says our names together as if we are one word.
No   space   between.
Sunset brings storybooks and rainbow striped pajamas
and she is getting too big for us both to fit side by side
in the rocking chair yet still we squeeze in anyway.
Something about listening to you sing her to sleep
always brings my heart up to my throat.
I look into her big blue eyes and see
everything good in this world.
I see endless possibilities, I see you.
When she remarks on how my necklace
is the moon and yours is the sun,
I want to tell her
she is every single star in the sky.
The whole entire galaxy.

SOLAR FLARE

Rainbow light through the morning blinds,
illuminating me in places I never thought
would see the sun again.
A light so cosmically bright
it almost blinds you.
Unable to see it sometimes, most times.
So I'll reflect it back to you,
scouring the town for every mirror I can find,
holding them up to say: "See? See your light now?"
Burning holes into the earth
until you see your own light, too.

IN LIKE A LION, BARING ITS TEETH

I've been sitting and staring at the dirt
trying to will spring to come.
There is mud under my fingernails
from trying to make things bloom
before they're ready.
I can't shake the feeling I'm teetering
on the edge of some giant precipice.
Something about the seasons changing
always feels like becoming.
I buy myself flowers and the scent
of roses is almost enough to trick me,
but I let them sit for too long
and they rot on the coffee table.
Timing has never been my strong suit.
I will try to keep my hands out of the garden.
The daisies will come soon.
I hope April will be kind.

SPRING IS A FIRST DATE & I'M FEELING FLIRTATIOUS

Something about this spring in particular feels like a first date with a stranger. She brings me flowers, a fragrant lilac bouquet wrapped in a promise. She is gentle and warm and smells of freshly washed linen hung to dry in the sun. I think I might like her, this May, but she is still a stranger and I am still apprehensive. Wind's whisper kisses the hair around my face and May says something about the birth of Venus. I try to hide the blush clawing its way up my throat.

I have been begging for a thawing since winter and now that it's finally here I don't know what to do with what I wished for. I know I should savor the tenderness of spring, however short-lived, before I am drowning in the heat of summer. Before July swallows me whole.

It can just be a little fling, nothing serious, but May reminds me I have never been good at casual. Wanting has always been my downfall. Perhaps this time I won't shy away, won't pretend to play it cool. I want the permanence of ink and I am not afraid to lay myself bare for it. Everything feels brand new in spring. The possibilities are endless but this time I want promises. Maybe this isn't the season for permanence. But if the flowers have taken root, why can't I?

SWIMMING LESSONS

Lately everything has been coming in waves. I suppose it always has, really. One minute I'm floating and the next I'm coughing up salt water on the bathroom floor.

I try to come back into my body, to be present. I do yoga. Go on walks. Hold my hands under ice water until they're red. My problem has always been that I exist too much in my head, and I don't really know how to get out.

It begins like a tide. A gentle tugging I can almost ignore until it pulls me under. There's really no choice but to follow. To wade in. It's up to my ankles, then my knees. Sand falls away from my heels, sucks me in. I can still breathe, tell myself I can still turn around if I want to. It's not too late. But the tide is stronger than I am, and I've never been one to deny the moon what she wants.

It happens in the bookstore, the grocery store, the parking lot. Safe places. Normal places. Places where I try to pretend I am just like everybody else. I place honeycrisp apples in my basket and wonder what happens to the ones with bruises. I hope somebody picks them. I hope somebody takes them home. I feel guilty for not being that somebody. Five minutes into the produce section and I am already failing.

Today the bookstore makes me feel like an exposed nerve. There are too many people, too much electricity confined in one space. Spine after spine blurs together in my brain, goes watery. Everyone is talking and laughing and I know it's not at me. It's not at me. There is fresh air in my lungs but salt water burning at the corners of my eyelids. Quick blinking. Quick walking. The tide is coming soon, and I have never been a very fast swimmer.

On Thursday I spend the morning coughing salt water into the life raft of my bedsheets. It takes four hours to get it all out. I tell myself I am allowed to stay in bed as long as I keep the blinds up, let the sunlight in. When my lungs are clear and I've wrung out the sheets, I leave to get a haircut. Just a little off the ends. Just the dead, unsightly bits. You can make the outside shiny enough to trick anyone with just a little trim. It looks healthier now, doesn't it?

I take a poetry workshop where the prompt is to write about the body. But don't they understand I still can't get out of my head? I get down three bullet points before my pen lifts from the page, breaking the cardinal rule. I cannot write about my body and I cannot write about the only thing I want to write about so I do not write at all. I eat two bites of chocolate ice cream from the orange ceramic dish. My cat whines when I won't let him lick the spoon. I move the dish, pat his head. Apologize for trying to keep him safe.

It's time to stop swimming against the current but I don't know how to unclench my fists, how to let it flow through me. I know only crescent moons on palms, only tension. There are beautiful things in the ocean, too. Glimmers of sunlight on the horizon. But this constant cycle of drowning and undrowning is a difficult one to break, and my legs and lungs are so tired. I just want to go home, but I'm not sure which direction to swim.

My bed is an island. My blankets, a weight to keep me close to shore. I wake two hours before I need to and the feeling floods me like a tap I can't turn off. I try not to wake my cat who lies unaware at the foot of my bed.

Even turning to my right is a reminder of amber leaves, of everything. I think I'd like to cancel today, pull the covers up over my head and go back. I know I will start to get tired again right before my alarm ticks. Just once I would like to get what I want when I want it.

RESURRECTION

October's sun hangs heavy in the sky
burning through lilac-rimmed clouds.
If I just keep driving, keep going,
will I be consumed by it, or fall
straight off the edge of the earth?
It would be so easy to let
my body be devoured.
Burnt up, spit out, reassembled.

These days I am less of a phoenix
and more like bear grass, which is to say
I do not rise from the ashes,
wings blazing, but grow slowly
out of charred dirt, taking my time.
A reminder that softness sometimes
comes from fire catching, if you let it.
If you give it time.

I think I've endured enough flames
to take as long as I need
to bloom again.

ACKNOWLEDGEMENTS

To my mom, thank you for your unwavering love and support.

To my amazingly talented community of writers from **WWC** and **WWIN**. You are all geniuses and I am so lucky to know each and every one of you. Thank you for making me feel safe enough to share the beginnings of this collection in our workshops.

To Jillian, for believing me and helping me say it out loud. Thank you for helping me heal.

To Carmen Maria Machado for writing *In the Dream House*. Your book was the first time I ever saw my experience reflected on the page. Thank you for sharing your truth and paving the way for me to share mine.

To Salem, for endless cuddles. I love you forever, even when you bite my nose.

To Dylah, for being the brightest sun in my galaxy. Thank you for being my partner both in work and in life. I can't imagine doing any of this without you by my side. I am so happy I left my heart open so you could find your way in.

To survivors, I see you and I believe you. You are so loved.

ABOUT THE AUTHOR

Becky Duffyhill Photography

Catherine Merritt is a writer and the manager of *Petals & Pages*, a queer and feminist independent bookstore in Denver, CO. Her work explores themes of lesbian identity, healing, and above all, love. *Gut the Ghost* is her debut poetry collection. You can follow Catherine on Instagram at @catherineinwords and on Substack at catherineinwords.substack.com.